Endorsements

"*Knowing Mr. Hardge the majority of my life, I have witnessed his manifestation into manhood. The personal experiences and reflections that he has shared with his readers, serve as a testimony of how one person can change his life and the lives of others. I personally applaud Mr. Hardge for his accomplishments, and for taking the time to share with readers; with the sincerest hope that other lives will be inspired.*"

Dennis Wright, President,
100 Black Men of Greater Fort Lauderdale, Fl

"*Prescription For Success, 17 Steps For Success and Achievement is a book that is truly necessary in our community. Adults will benefit, but it will prove to be extraordinarily beneficial in the hands and minds of those approaching adulthood, and young boys and girls. Reading this book can radically expedite our drive towards individuality, family, cultural and community Success. Great Job Mr. Hardge!*"

Louis Oliver
Former Miami Dolphin

"*Prescription For Success is a must read! Mr. Hardge delivers profound principles that will propel its readers personally and professionally to championship status.*"

Vernon J. Shazier, Executive Pastor,
Mount Bethel Ministries
Fort Lauderdale, Fl

"*Prescription For Success is brilliantly written. Mr. Hardge consciously crafts the need to succeed with the need to read, and how mentoring is a vital component to internal development of our youth. This Prescription For Success can clearly be used as a road map that can be used to align the minds of our youth and adults with goal setting and achievement.*"

Willie Brown,
Polemarch, Alumni Chapter
Kappa Alpha Psi Fraternity, Inc
Pompano Beach, Fl

"Our society has become filled with individuals who idolize movie stars, sports figures and musicians. Mr. Hardge is a true hero, because his life is a testimony of hard work, dedication, and spiritual revelation. His book and music reflect an individual who understands, to truly accomplish anything in life; you must do your best and let God do the rest. However, success is not the only thing that will follow, ultimately your life will have a positive impact on others. His propelling book, "Prescription For Success" is a thought provoking book that illustrates the intangibles for Success. He will be a motivating force and example to people of all ages."

Odessa Bennett
Alpha Kappa Alpha Sorority, Inc.
Zeta Rho Omega Chapter
Fort Lauderdale, Florida
Nominating Committee Member and Silver Star
(25 years Plus Member)

"Mr. Hardge has managed to inject his personal life experiences and achievements as a point of reference for authenticating the writing of Prescription For Success. The contents of this book are a blend of brightness and spirit that provide a solution for life's challenges and adversities. A flash of revelation for the solutions to problems we face on daily basis; a subconscious message that conveys a course of conduct; a moment of brilliance; a revelation of wisdom. Mr. Hardge makes it loud and clear that success comes from knowing what you want, not wanting what you know. He has mixed this formula with success, a sprinkling of hierarchy, worship, faith, and a set of beliefs and tenets. He explains the need to combine your faith, and upward mobility with a strong set of ethics; a proper behavior for all individuals towards themselves and others. Mr. Hardge has provided a guide, an insight for wanting and achieving success."

Tyson Jones,
Former City Commissioner
City of Lauderhill, FL

PRESCRIPTION FOR SUCCESS

MR. HARDGE

Distinct Publishers

Distinct Publishers

StarGroup International
www.stargroupinternational.com

FIRST EDITION

Edited by Gwen Carden
Cover and book design by Mel Abfier

Printed in Korea

Library of Congress Cataloging-in-Publication Data pending

Prescription for Success - Mr. Hardge

ISBN 978-0-615-21836-6

Table of contents

FOREWORD

*P*rescription For Success is an intellectual, inspirational, and informative approach to holistic success. Mr. Hardge is a custom made gift to this generation. The concepts and principles provided in this book are not only life challenging, but life changing.

In Prescription For Success, you will find several principles that will serve as ingredients for achievement. Each principle is concise, and an invaluable lesson with specific techniques for internal development, which will create external accomplishments.

Mr. Hardge has methodically disarmed mediocrity and the spirit of deprivation. Prepare to soar, and welcome the spirit of excellence.

We are forever indebted to Mr. Hardge for having the vision and courage to write this book.

Read it and excel!!!!!

Pastor Torrey Phillips
Gospel of Christ Church
Fort Lauderdale, Fl

ACKNOWLEDGEMENTS

irst and foremost I must thank God for all of the blessings he has bestowed upon me. The biggest one being my Lord and Savior Jesus Christ, for it is through him that all things are possible. A thank you that grows exponentially to John and Virginia Hardge, for the strongest part of the tree is the root. To my rib, Moni and my kids, Darrielle, Dominique, Darrell, Dylan, I draw my inspiration from all of you. To the rest of the Hardge Family (HMI), we did it! A special thanks to my Spiritual Warriors who have made an endless amount of spiritual deposits within me. Pastor Wayne Lomax, Pastor Gregory Bernard Pope, Dr. C.E. Glover, Dr. Mack King Carter, Pastor Ed Brinson, Reverend Stanley, Bishop Victor Curry, Pastor Amos Benefield, Minister Vernon Shazier, Pastor Anderson, Pastor Torrey Phillips. To My Spiritual Warriors in other states: Bishop Eddie Long, Pastor TD Jakes, Bishop Noel Jones, Dr. Creflo Dollar, Dr. A.R. Bernard, Dr. Leroy Thompson, Pastor Paul S. Morton. I want to thank all of you for making a difference in my life, and you probably did not even know it. May God keep shinning through you, so we can see! A humungous thanks goes out to the faculty at St. Bernadette Catholic School of Hollywood, Collins Elementary School, William Dandy (formerly Everglades MS), Boyd Anderson High School, Tampa Tech Institute and Florida Memorial College. For Education is the foundation of Success. A shout out to The Brothers of

Kappa Alpha Psi Fraternity Incorporated, Pop, Crunchy, Kirby, Nard, June, Tony, Maurice, Zack, Lil Rick, Mike Williams, and everybody from 21st. Rest in Peace Fat Floyd, Tim Fain, Tony Simms, and to all of my fallen Soldiers who died in the struggle. To all of my homeboys from Ft. Lauderdale, Lauderdale Lakes, Royal Palm, Westwood, Parkway, Dillard Homes, Lauderdale Manors, Lauderhill, Deepside, Shallowside, Dania, Hallandale, Hollywood, Pompano, Deerfield. My family in the 305 and 561 area codes and all of my folks who moved to the Atlanta area. A special thanks to Coach Johnny Alexander from the Western Tigers and Coach Nelson Gonzalez from Lauderdale Lakes Vikings. To Coach Big Jim Parker from Florida Memorial University, May you Rest in Peace. Thanks to every person who is a coach. I am living proof that your efforts are not in vain.

Mr. Hardge

A
WORD FROM THE AUTHOR

*M*y mission is to provide clear concepts and principles that will serve as the ingredients for your success.

Your time is the single most important element in helping you achieve success in any endeavor. When we are born it is only a matter of time before we die. Therefore, the most important aspect of life is how we spend the time between the moment we are born and the moment we die. Why waste something that can never be replaced? Your time is the one thing that gives you an opportunity to create that which you desire. Most of the things obtained in life require time to be achieved. We trade time and labor in return for a salary or wages. We trade time and effort in exchange for love. We take time to discipline children so they will grow up to be disciplined individuals. We must exchange time and action to remain physically fit. If time is removed from any of these examples, nothing can be successfully achieved. How you spend your time today will determine how you live your life tomorrow.

Mentorship is another Key to Success

Greatness begets greatness. Surround yourself with others more experienced than you so you can learn while remaining humble. It is also your responsibility to surround yourself with individuals, mentees, who can benefit from the relationships you have with your mentors. This will provide you with leadership opportunities and give you clarity. Each one teach one! Your mentor should be your Model of Excellence. Having a model who strives for excellence is significant in achieving your goals. A Model for Excellence is someone who can be trusted, based on their inner strength, character, knowledge and level of skill and ability. It is not someone perfect, but rather someone who is well grounded. This individual should be able to provide insight into situations you face and provide alternatives and solutions to unforeseen obstacles. This person provides open opportunities for dialogue and cares more about your future than your present situation. It takes a good man to create his own success, but it takes a great man to create the rest.

The Power of Learning

Most of us are not wealthy because our ancestors were not wealthy or financially independent. It is almost impossible to get what you don't know. Achieving and keeping financial independence requires reading books and surrounding yourself with people who are financially independent and working hard and smart. We must seek business opportunities that provide access to products and services that will create wealth. One must learn wealth and success principles and apply what one has learned in order to become successful and wealthy. Learning is one of the key elements to becoming successful in any area.

Florida Memorial College, 1991

INTRODUCTION

The picture you see on the previous page was taken in 1991. I was a 21 year old freshman at Florida Memorial College, now Florida Memorial University. "Flo-Mo" was definitely better than the place I might have ended up had I not changed my ways. In the late 80's and early 90's my community became infected with an enormous amount of drugs, guns, and violence. Unfortunately, the pressures of life back then caused me to make some bad decisions, and I am not particularly proud of them today. However, it is by the Grace of God that I am still here, and I am thankful to be able to utilize my past experiences to provide insight to those who may need direction. Coming up as a youth in this climate provided me with opportunities and affiliates that were new for me. I was what they called green, but the streets have a way of teaching you to grow up real fast.

Growing up in the streets of Ft. Lauderdale taught me lessons that I will never forget, and the old adage is true, "If you hang with dogs, you will eventually get fleas." In my case, I was hanging with individuals who had a sincere fetish for accumulating money. We know them as hustlers. As I take a glimpse into my past at the chances I took, I think I was simply functioning out of carelessness, immaturity and ignorance. I was young and thought the street life was fun and exciting. I never thought that the consequences of my actions could have cost me my life. Most of my comrades shared the same goals: get rich or die trying. However, my life began to change when some of my comrades actually started dying trying to get rich. Suddenly, the street life and getting rich was no longer appealing. Well, I still wanted to get rich,

"A failure establishes only
this, that our determination
to succeed was not strong
enough."

John Christian Bovee

but I had to find another route. When I learned to value my life more than anything else, I left the streets behind me and went to college.

Florida Memorial University served as the cocoon in my life cycle. The Butterfly Theory states that we all begin life as caterpillars, and if we are going to continue to grow throughout life, we have to go through some changes. These changes are similar to a caterpillar going through a metamorphosis within the cocoon. After a period of time, which varies for each individual, we become strong enough to fight our way out of the cocoon, and finally spread our wings as a butterfly. We could not have accomplished going from a caterpillar to a butterfly without change. At Florida Memorial I learned the difference between being proactive and being reactive. In other words, if I studied for the test (proactive), I wouldn't have to cheat or cram to pass (reactive).

In 1991 I managed to make the varsity basketball team as a walk-on in exchange for a free education. In addition to making the team, I met some wonderful people and created new relationships as I focused my attention on growing up, not just growing older. I monitored my thoughts, because I realized my thoughts would become my actions, my actions would become my habits, my habits would create my character, and my character would determine my future. By 1996 my mission was accomplished. Approximately five years after entering the gates of FMU, I had transformed into a new being. However, I realized that if I wanted to continue grow spiritually and mentally, it would be a lifelong process.

In May of 1996 I graduated with a Bachelors of Science Degree in Computer Science. Leaving the street life behind me was challenging but necessary. Florida Memorial University provided me with an opportunity to continue to re-create my image of myself, my self identity. I was willing to change my thoughts, because I wanted to change my life.

A few months after graduation, Broward County Public Schools hired me as a Computer Teacher at McNicol Middle School in Hollywood, Florida. My starting salary was around $30,000 per year, which was plenty for me at that time in my life. Darrielle, my daughter, was six years old and my only real responsibility outside of myself. The head basketball coaching position at the school became available, and it was a perfect fit. People had been making deposits of encouragement, direction, and inspiration into my life since I could remember, and it was time for me to deposit seeds of encouragement, direction, and inspiration into the live of others.

However, I had financial goals I wanted to attain, and it would have been difficult to accomplish them in the profession I was in. Mixed emotions plagued my mind because I wanted to assist in the development of the children I came in contact with on a daily basis, but money was on my mind, and I wanted a piece of the American Dream as well.

After reviewing my salary progression for the next twenty years in the school system, I had to make a decision. It would have taken me approximately 15 years to earn a salary of $50,000 teaching, and I wanted to make millions. Not to have for myself, but to help others. See, I always wanted to be a Philanthropist. A Philanthropist is an individual who makes financial contributions to worthy causes, one who focuses on increasing the well-being of mankind, by charitable aid or donations. However, in order to give away a lot of money and help others, you first must have it to give. The real reason that one is blessed is to be a blessing. We are mere vessels that God uses to enrich the lives of those with whom we come in contact. My mind was on money, and money was on my mind! Immediately, the search for another position and additional money became the priority, but I begin to think about a purpose for living, outside of just earning money.

After work one day, a friend from my old neighborhood named Randall Jones asked me to attend a meeting with him at the home of Tylus and Yvonne Grant. Their son Troy and I grew up playing football for the Western Tigers under the leadership of Coach Johnny Alexander in the late 70's and early 80's. We were close friends then and remain so to this day. Mr. and Mrs. Grant were successful black business owners and pioneers in our community, I mean just good people. Sitting inside the Grant Estate, Troy began talking about making big money thanks to the deregulation of the telecommunications industry, and utilizing multi-level marketing as a vehicle to become financially independent. It made sense to me, and I signed up that night. One week later we attended an American Communications Network (ACN) briefing at the Holiday Inn on Highway 441 in Ft. Lauderdale. I felt invigorated the moment I entered the room, like this was where I was supposed to be. Here was a business opportunity that had the potential to allow me to accomplish my life-long dream of becoming a Philanthropist. It lit a fire inside of me that is still burning today. That fire is called education. I realized for the first time that the key to my success in this endeavor, or any other, was to educate myself as much as possible about the business. Over the next six months we traveled to Atlanta, Georgia, and Charlotte, North Carolina networking with men and women earning over $30,000 a month. Most were young African-Americans, and I realized that if they could do it, so could I.

Reko Enterprises consisted of two brothers from Ft. Lauderdale who had moved to Atlanta. They were introduced to the ACN Opportunity and, in turn, came back to Ft. Lauderdale to begin sharing this opportunity with others. There was an awful lot of money involved in ACN, but it came with a price. That price was learning, and then applying what you learned to create what you earned. Growth meant allowing oneself to be placed in new and challenging situations, and learning to be comfortable in them. I heard several individuals speaking about re-educating themselves on how to be successful. That re-education and the application of what they learned put them in a financial position to leave their jobs, and it made sense to me. If we have to work, why not work at being wealthy? It only took me 60 days to rise to the first corporately earned position within the company, Executive Field Trainer. However, that didn't mean I was making a lot of money.

To be perfectly honest, I did not make a lot of money with ACN, but I continued to change. ACN was another cocoon in the life cycle. My attitude, attire, dialogue, and habits began to align with getting to the top position in the company, Regional Vice President, (RVP). More importantly, I was becoming a better person inwardly. Chris Oliver, Montrell Jackson, Delxino Wilson DeBriano, Robert Dean and Herschel Gibbs were leaders within our organization and they inspired me. These brothers not only dressed to a T, but they were smart. They realized that in order to be successful, you had to do what the successful people do. Reading was an integral part of their daily routines. They shared their success habits with me, and the torch was passed. I envisioned myself on the stage just like them. I wanted to share this opportunity with everybody I came into contact with. I was excited, not only because of the possibilities of becoming financially independent, but also because it allowed me to understand if I changed my mind or my thoughts, my life would change. It also taught me the principal that if you help others get what they want out of life, you would automatically get what you want. If we want good things to come out of life, we have to make sure we put good things into it.

Before I knew it, they asked me to begin facilitating their business briefings. Who would have thought that I would be on stage speaking in front

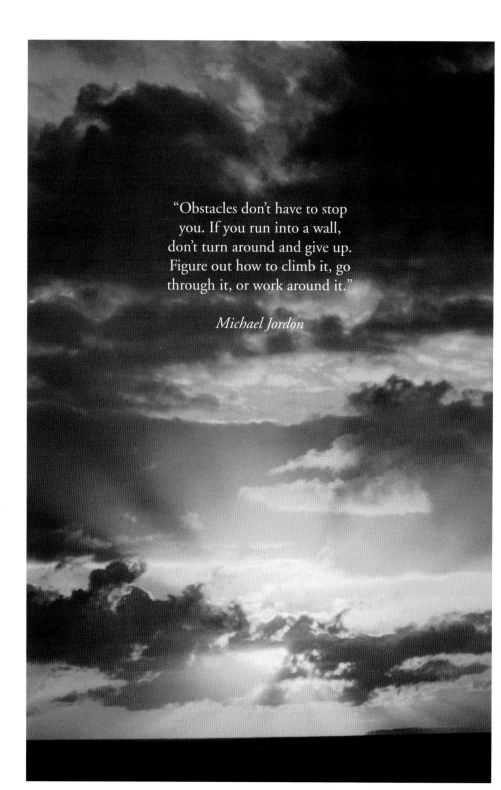

"Obstacles don't have to stop you. If you run into a wall, don't turn around and give up. Figure out how to climb it, go through it, or work around it."

Michael Jordon

of hundreds of people about how they could become financially independent? I would! Envisioning myself speaking at these meetings was a constant for me. I replayed the mental picture in my mind over and over and over again, because that is what I had a desire to do. The picture was so vivid and clear that it forced its way into reality. Every individual becomes what they are due to the dominant thought that they allow to occupy their mind.

Earning is directly proportional to applying what you learn. Adopting the mindset of a multi-millionaire was easy for me because I was always smart, and I had envisioned myself having a shipload of money from an early age. I didn't want the money just to horde for myself, but to let others know that God gave all of us the ability to get wealth (Deuteronomy 8:18). Since he gave us the ability, we may as well utilize our abilities to get it, and enrich his Kingdom.

I still was teaching, it was just teaching a different subject. Instead of teaching computers and basketball, it was wealth, prosperity, and abundance via the deregulation of the telecommunications industry. Bigger than anything, I found my gift for teaching, which led me to my purpose for living. ACN did not provide the financial reward for me, but it prepared me for the financial reward. It taught me the importance of having a positive relationship with God, people, and money. I began reading books on successful people and attending wealth seminars. The topics of prosperity and wealth were common in our organizational meetings, and we shared our dreams and desires often because we believed in ourselves and each other.

In December of 1998, I was hired as a Customer Service Analyst III by Education Technology Services, (ETS) the Technology Department within Broward County Public Schools. My starting salary was $42,000 per year, and that was a $12,000 increase from my teaching salary.

I was appreciative to get the position. However, it was not until dividing $12,000 by 12 months in a year did I realize it was only an additional $1,000 a month. Big dreams and aspirations would not let me get comfortable. Thankful, but not fulfilled, appreciative, but not settling, was my motto.

Working at ETS under the direction of Kathy Collins and Dr. Jeanine Gendron was rewarding. My primary responsibility was to assist Regina Ferrazzo with the Technology Liaison Contact Program. A few years later, Regina was transferred to the Human Resource Management Systems Department, and my title became Technology Liaison Contact Coordinator.

Technology Liaison Contacts are individuals hired at each school/department to maintain the technology at their locations. There were approximately 300 TLCs in the district, and I arranged monthly meetings with them in the North, North Central, South, South Central, and District areas of the Broward County Public Schools System. These meetings would provide them with technology-related information and Results Driven Staff Development to assist them in their daily responsibilities. I really enjoyed working with the TLCs in Broward County Public Schools. They are a wonderful group of people.

In 2000, the organization that I created in ACN slowed and finally dwindled away. However, there was something in me that did not stop. I tried other business opportunities, but they were lacking something. ACN had made me think about a purpose for living in addition to becoming financially independent. Each of us is created with our own individual purpose and intent, and the only one who can assist us in finding the purpose and intent of our creation is the one who created us. It is through prayer and reading the Basic Instructions Before Leaving Earth (BIBLE), that we will find ourselves in His will.

Life is intended for us to live, not to merely exist. The jungle is the domain of a lion. That is where this species was created and is intended to be. The ocean is the domain of a Killer Whale. That is where it was created and is intended to be. That is where they are free to live. A zoo is simply a place where the lion and the killer whale exist. So it is with us. Most of us are just like animals in a zoo, confined within the barriers of our minds and failing to realize that we are free to reach our full potential. The sky is truly the limit if you have not placed limitations on yourself. Are you trapped in the zoo of life? If so, break out. You can do more than merely exist. You are alive, so live.

In life, we must align ourselves with a purpose that is bigger than ourselves. My purpose is to understand God's purpose for my life and share my experiences and what I have learned along the way with everyone who will listen. Becoming a Philanthropist and teaching about the goodness of God, the fruits of the spirit, health, wealth, prosperity and success are my main objectives. Becoming financially independent and self-sufficient was and still is very important to me. I replay these words over and over in my mind. The picture is vivid and precise. I wish to empower those who have an inward desire for more. I want you to realize you can attain it, if you are willing to grow in order to receive it. Learning to want more for the right reasons is imperative.

The one thing I realized back then is that success often goes against the norm. If you want what most people don't have, you have to do what most people don't do. Most people can't fathom owning an airplane or helicopter. Most people can't imagine owning a home in Jamaica, Miami, New York and California. Most people can't see themselves living to this capacity and therefore will not. Success and achievement begin in the mind, the information we feed our minds formulates thoughts, and thoughts become things. Whatever the mind of a man can conceive and believe, it can achieve.

As a man thinketh in his heart, so is he (Proverbs 23:7)

The Proverb above works pertaining to wealth as well as poverty. Whatever the mind of a man can conceive and believe, it can achieve. We have the opportunity of a lifetime every day above ground. We must strive to be the best we can be by having an attitude of greatness and gratitude. However, we can't fool ourselves. We know deep down inside if we are really willing to work towards accomplishing our dreams, it is not a travesty to die without accomplishing them. The travesty lies in dying without having any dreams to accomplish.

In 2002, I started investing in real estate and by 2006 had generated over $1 million in real estate revenue for Hardge Management Incorporated. Our business plan centered on buying vacant pieces of land, building single family homes on the land, and selling them within the black community. The Principles I learned in ACN years before prepared me for that moment in time.

The principles set forth in this book are life-changing, but you have to be ready to change for life. The words and thoughts we choose to allow to harbor in our minds will create images, and these images will be reflected in our actions, habits, and ultimately will shape our future. We must think positively and work towards becoming the individual we see inside the deep crevices of our minds. We must focus on the idea or the person we wish to become and formulate a definitive plan in order for the idea or person to manifest. God gave the birds of the air worms to eat, but he did not put the worms in the nest because if he placed the worms in the nest, the bird might never leave and would not learn to fly. Now that goes against the very nature of a bird. Its purpose is to fly. If a bird did not fly, we would assume something was wrong with that bird. So it is with us being successful. The mere fact we are alive gives us the opportunity to accomplish whatever we are willing to pay the price to accomplish. Nothing is impossible. The word impossible means I'm Possible.

For we can do all things through Christ, who strengthens us
(Philippians 4:13)

At the beginning of 2007, the real estate market was not doing as well as we had anticipated, and I found myself back at the drawing board. From 2002 to 2007 real estate was my bridge over trouble waters. By November 2007, it seemed as if the bridge had run out and nobody had warned me. I had several pieces of property that I decided not to build on because so many homes were going into foreclosure and it was getting difficult for buyers to secure financing. Hundreds of banks went out of business, and that had a significant impact of my business. Real Estate will always be a part of my financial portfolio, but I was at a point in life where I needed some immediate changes. As things got progressively worse I began writing Prescription for Success and recording the musical aspect of the project. By the Summer of 2008 my book and the CD were ready for the world. When things get tight, we are often squeezed into positions that are meant to bring out the best in us. There is an old adage that says "When the going gets tough, the tough get going." Remember, in order to grow through life, you must change. Your Life Cycle has a stage in it called the Cocoon; this is where the metamorphosis or change takes place. Embrace this phase of life, because this is where you will get your wings to fly.

Even though I was no longer in business with Reggie and Erik Kennon, the relationship we established back then created a bond that ventures beyond business, and that bond is based on a common purpose. They are currently involved in Tahitian Noni and doing very well working with Robert Dean, Herchell Gibbs, and Barry Bird. We were in ACN together years ago, and they stayed with multi-level marketing and finally made it big.

Robert Dean is the brainchild behind TOPGUN International, an affiliate of Tahitian Noni International, and is one of the leading money earners in the company. Mr. Dean wrote a book called, *The Dean Effect* and recently created his own Success Magazine. The magazine chronicles the Success his organization is having by utilizing Tahitian Noni International as a vehicle to create healthy and wealthy lifestyles.

I AM

INFORMATION+APPLICATION=MANIFESTATION

*I*nformation is the single most important aspect of our society. Education serves to provide individuals the proper information in various subjects so they can make informed decisions. This is truly where success begins, for without the proper information you will not achieve the proper manifestation. Once you have the proper information, you need the proper application to render the proper manifestation. This principle is simple, yet profound. I am what I know and can apply. If we knew what Donald Trump and Robert Kiyosaki knew, and did what they did, we would have what they have. However, the reason we don't have what they have is that we don't do what they do, because we don't know what they know. It all begins with what one knows, Information.

It is the application of what I know that determines what I am. It is that which was planted that is creating the results. The only way to change the result is to change what was planted. Get your shovel and start digging out the roots of unproductiveness in your life and replace them with seeds of productivity (such as success books, successful role models, CDs, DVD's, etc.), seeds of positive thinking, seeds of preparation, planning and leadership. Everything we read, watch or listen to is a seed. The only difference is the type of seed being planted.

The only way to change tomorrow is by changing what we do today!

What is Success?

Success is not just about having money, material possessions or status. True Success contributes to the development of an individual's character. The spiritual, mental, emotional, physical and financial development of an individual creates an internal balance. This balance contributes to the Success of this individual because they have developed internally.

Elizabeth Towne stated, "Success is having the ability to liberally command what one desires with a clear conscience and a loving heart." It can also be as simple as setting a goal and accomplishing it, the manifestation of an idea, the end result of action steps taken to accomplish a goal or objective. Success is the end result of exercising your faith and your labor. There can be no success if there is no labor. It is nearly impossible to go through life thinking one can become successful if one does not labor.

Success is the ability to make decisions based on personal beliefs, not lack of money, politics, fear or guilt. Success is the ability to wake up in the morning inspired and go to bed at night with peace of mind, the ability to have the ways, means, time and guts to choose and follow your own path. Success is the ability share love, be filled with purpose, passion, and fun in life, and being healthy in body, mind and spirit. Success is the ability to use your unique gifts in a way that makes a positive difference in the lives of many people. It is the ability to inspire and motivate others, to make people laugh – including yourself.

Success is knowing that you're on the right path and not alone in your journey. Success is understanding that "getting there" isn't half the fun, it's most of it. It's the ability to make the most of what you've been given, to take advantage of every opportunity and face every fear, and to understand the difference between existing and living.

Success is much more than money! It is growing through life, not going through life. Utilizing information to propel you towards success. This is not the end-all, tell-all manual for success, but the information encompassed within these pages has contributed immensely towards my internal development and growth. Success is a journey, not a destination. Success is about change.

Success Tips:

1. Preparation

It is better to be prepared for an opportunity and not have one, than to have an opportunity and not be prepared for one. We must prepare for the expected outcomes the future holds. The decisions we made in the past brought us into our present position in life, and the decisions we make in the present will determine the future. Today's actions are the seeds that will produce tomorrow's fruit.

2. Internal Development

We as human beings live in three spheres: mind, body, and spirit, and we possess a soul. Developing these different, yet integral, parts of our existence is crucial. Sekou Toure, President of Guinea, defines the Science of Dehumanization as the process of indoctrinating you against yourself by denying internal development for external reward. If we allocate a majority of our time developing the body and fail to develop the mind and spirit, our body becomes the rudder of our lives. If we spend most of our time developing the flesh, the flesh makes decisions that are oftentimes not in accordance with the mind and the spirit. When I say developing the flesh, I mean reading, watching, and actively participating in activities that feed the fleshly aspects of our lives. We must pay attention to all three aspects of our lives to make sure we are feeding them proportionately. Balance is one of the keys to opulence. When one spends a majority of his time developing the mind and the spirit, the body must follow their lead. Exercise, health and wellness are vital for success, but pay close attention to the internal aspects of your existence — your spirit, your soul, your will, your determination, your drive and motivation - all the intangibles that create the tangible. For it is that which is internal that will manifest. Get ready.

Johann Wolfgang von Goethe said, "If we treat others as if they were what they ought to be, we may assist them in becoming what they are capable of being."

3. Proper Application leads to Increase

In the past I was led to believe the statement, "Knowledge is power." Well, this statement is partially true. Knowledge is potential power, and once the potential power is applied, then comes the manifestation of the application. It is the application of what one knows that leads to the creation of something. Simply knowing creates nothing. The same is true pertaining to the accumulation of money. It is the application of what one learns that determines what one earns. Therefore, we must first learn, then apply what we learn to receive the fruits of the application.

It is in the learning process that we begin to understand how to deal with the manifestation of the application, which brings us to the word "preparation." We must train or prepare every day as if the championship were tomorrow. Will you be ready when your number is called? Will you be ready to make the game-winning shot? Will you be ready to deal with the blessings you have been praying for? You will if preparation is and has been the focal point of your life. You should always be preparing for what life has in store for you. In other words, if you desire increase, immerse yourself in the information in the area that you desire to increase in. Matthew 6:33 says, "Seek ye first the kingdom of God, and his righteousness; and all these things shall be added unto you." Acquire literature, tapes, CDs and DVDs to provide the proper information to assist with the increase you desire. It is natural to desire increase. Feed your mind and stimulate your spirit. You must feed your seeds. Our thoughts are the seeds of our lives. Therefore, feed your mind with the information you need to propel you towards increase. Seeds need nourishment in order to germinate. Feed your thoughts, apply what you learn, and watch your thoughts turn into reality.

YOUR DECISIONS DECIDE YOUR WEALTH

*J*ust about everyone wants more out of life. The most important aspect in the accumulation of money is having a specific goal to move towards. This will allow one the ability to monitor their decisions, which will create their actions. Every decision will create an action that will take one closer to accomplishing a goal, or further away. There is something burning on the inside of us that keeps wanting more, and there is not a single thing wrong with wanting all that life has to give. But you are going to have to be willing to give all that you have to get it, while maintaining a certain level of integrity. Integrity is making decisions with a moral, ethical, biblical, and legal perspective.

If more money is what you desire, then make sure the financial decisions are aligned with your goal. Do not allow looking rich to become a barrier to becoming rich. This was a lesson I learned the hard way. Between 2002 and 2006 I made more money than I ever had in my life. I had saved a significant amount of money and paid my bills off for an entire year. My mortgage, car notes, insurances, you name it. Every major monthly expense I paid off for one year, which kept my monthly expenditures low. In theory, this was a perfect plan, because every three months I was supposed to sell one of the newly constructed homes and make $25-30,000. We had ten to 15 homes to build, so I basically purchased whatever I thought I could afford. These purchases created a significant amount of debt that I did not see, because it was paid off for the year. The real estate plan I created was supposed to last until 2011, but the real estate industry had a mind of its own. I was making good money, but I was creating more debt as I made more money. For example, in 2005, I acquired a 2005 BMW 745i, a 2005 BMW X5 for my wife, and a 2005 Ford F150 for construction purposes, and in 2004 a $500,000 home. My wife and I went on shopping sprees, vacations and nights on the town. I mean we were living it up. Why not? I worked hard for my money. By the end of 2007, I had accumulated a lot of stuff and ran out of money. My monthly expenses reached an excess of $12,000, and I had dwindled my savings paying bills. In addition, I had several vacant pieces of land I couldn't build on because of the state of the real estate market, and that became additional debt that came looking for me every 30 days. That is when it hit me. Don't let looking rich become a barrier to becoming rich. If I had maintained a modest lifestyle, I could probably have weathered the storm a little better than I did. Having this kind of money was new to me, and I had to learn the hard way how to manage it. I went from making 3,000 a month working in a salaried job to over $10,000 a month as a future real estate mogul. Suddenly I faced all of the cars being repossessed and possibly a foreclosure on our home. I was down, but I was not beaten.

Most of the wealthy have experienced financial challenges at least once before making it big. I've read stories of several multi-millionaires filing bankruptcy and still making it to the top. Therefore, despite this setback I was determined to make it. I learned that a bend in the road becomes the end of the road if you fail to make the turn. Reading the stories of others assisted me in dealing with my current situation. I began to understand that this was just a part of the financial growth process. Plus, I got the lesson, and the next time I accumulated this type of money, I would make disciplined decisions pertaining to my business affairs. Sometimes experience is the best teacher, but we should not have to fall down and bump our heads every time to get the lesson. We must educate ourselves in the areas of creating wealth, financial planning, and seek the counsel of those who are already educated in those areas.

Remember, don't let looking rich become a barrier to becoming rich. Become rich, and then you will not have to worry about how you look, because you will be it. You can obtain anything you want if you are willing to pay the price for it. Becoming good at a particular sport costs. Buying a new home costs. Becoming educated costs. Everything you desire has a price. Whether it is financial or time, it is going to cost you something. An exchange has to take place in order to obtain it. The question is, are you willing to pay the price and make an exchange to get it?

Discipline is one of the major keys to Success.

SUCCESS LIES IN YOUR DAILY ROUTINES

ne thing is for certain: everyone gets 24 hours in a day and 365 days in a year. It is what one does with the time that determines what one accomplishes.

It seems as if we have become a society content with being entertained versus becoming educated. Don't get me wrong, entertainment is part of relaxation and a necessity in life. However, if more time is spent being entertained than working towards your goal, one will reap the seed of being entertained. Fill in the blanks below to determine how much of your valuable time is actually being spent working towards accomplishing your goals in a 24 hour day.

How many are spent working or going to school?
How many sleeping?
How many relaxing, listening to music or watching TV?
How many working out?
How many hours are spent casually on the computer?
How many hours are spent talking or communicating with your friends on the phone or email?
How many hours are spent hanging out with your friends at the mall or on the beach?

How many working on your goal?

How many going to church?

How many hours are spent feeding your mind the information needed to be successful in you area of interest?

How much time is spent attending events, workshops or taking classes that will assist you in becoming the person you want to become?

You have to structure your life and prioritize your time to maximize your ability to create your future. It takes time to create your future. Building your future is like building a house. The amount of time you spend planning and working will determine how long it takes you to complete it.

How much time are you willing to spend to build your house, which is your future? What we allocate our time to on a daily basis will determine what happens tomorrow. What we do today will determine where we are tomorrow. We must focus on our goals and work on them daily for our goals to manifest.

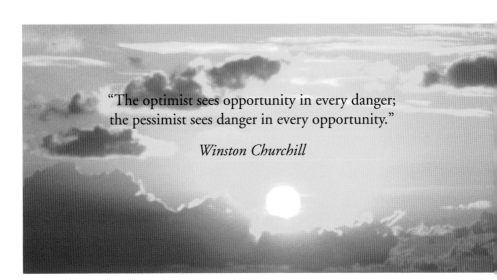

"The optimist sees opportunity in every danger; the pessimist sees danger in every opportunity."

Winston Churchill

CIRCLE OF COUNSEL

*N*ever discuss problems with someone incapable of solving them. What sense does it make to talk to someone who is single about marriage problems? Would you want to get advice about financial problems from someone who is broke? Does it make sense to seek scientific information from a classmate who is failing science? You need to find the individual making good grades in the subject. It is not only impractical but dangerous to seek counsel from an old drinking buddy about wanting to stop drinking. He is more likely to offer you a drink than give sound advice about stopping.

Ask and you will be given what you ask for. Seek, and you will find. Knock, and the door will be opened. For everyone who asks, receives. Anyone who seeks, finds. If only you will knock, the door will open. (Matthew 7:7-8)

GIGO
GARBAGE IN GARBAGE OUT!

An acronym commonly used in the computer industry is GIGO, which stands for Garbage In/Garbage Out. It simply means, whatever you put in the computer (input), will correspond with what comes out of the computer (output). The same can be applied to the human brain. Whatever we feed our minds will ultimately be displayed via our dialect, language, conversation and actions. You can tell what a person reads or takes in (input) by what he says, displays, or how he conducts himself (output). Our mind is like a sponge absorbing water. When the sponge is removed from the water and squeezed, water exudes. The brain is similar to this sponge, only it absorbs information. If you feed your mind positive information, it will generate a positive attitude, a positive outlook on life and a positive conversation. What we listen to and watch feeds the subconscious mind and will ultimately have an effect on how we live our lives.

The body has two entry gates to the mind, the ears and the eyes. Whatever we feed our mind by listening or watching will ultimately get into our heart, and out of the heart come the issues of life. If you want to change your life, you have to change your thoughts. If you want to change your thoughts, you have to change the information you allow into your mind. Change what you watch and listen to, and you will change your life.

As a man thinketh in his heart, so is he (Proverbs 23:7)

PEOPLE DON'T PLAN TO FAIL,
THEY FAIL TO PLAN!

In most successful situations and circumstances, plans are developed to ensure certain goals and objectives are reached. Man learned to plan early in his evolution. Throughout history, plans have consistently been formulated in order to successfully complete a task or accomplish a feat. In athletics, coaches call plays or plans that are designed to score points or stop the opponent from scoring. When taking a trip or a vacation, a map (plan) is necessary to get to the destination. Every building requires a set of plans prior to construction. At every educational institution, teachers devise lesson plans, and the educational institution has a syllabus (plan) stating what will be covered in that particular course. Success rarely happens by osmosis. In most cases, it is achieved by knowing what is desired and creating a way of getting it. Plans are essential for success, and success comes from following a plan.

Planning is the key to the future. Monitoring your actions will determine how close you come to accomplishing your goals. Each step you take should be calculated and precise to make sure you are going in the right direction. Ten minor occurrences can create a major one, so pay attention to the details and the minor occurrences. We often find ourselves in situations where we are surrounded by people who know more than we do about a particular subject or state of affairs. We must learn to use their brains for our gain. If it took someone years to learn how to open and operate a successful business, why not capitalize on their knowledge and experience to save yourself some time? Most people are willing to help someone who is willing to help themselves. Why? Maybe this poem can answer the question.

No man is an island
Nobody travels alone
The things we bring into the lives of others
Comes back into our own
-Unknown-

To structure your future you must plan and follow instructions. Why is it important to follow instructions?

I have come to realize that my success depends on my ability to evaluate my life and answer each one of the questions Diana Ross asked in her hit theme song from the 1975 film Mahogany, "Do you know where you are going to? Do you like the things life is showing you? What are you going through? Do you know?"

Your words and actions should serve as the engines propelling you towards your goal. If you are unable to answer each of these questions definitively, you need to listen to the track from my Prescription for Success CD entitled How to Get Ahead. You must find a purpose for living. If you don't like the circumstances you are in, change your thoughts. Your thoughts will change your actions, and you will change your circumstances.

A-BOX THEORY

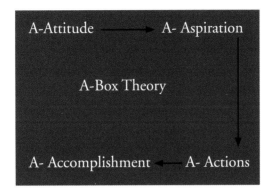

Your Attitude, what you think.
Will determine your Aspirations, what you desire.
Will determine your Actions, what you do.
Will determine your Accomplishments, what you get.

A-Box Theory is a universal principle that can be implemented to manifest ideas. Often life can be simplified if we learn not to overcomplicate situations. Our attitude is what we think or how we feel about something or someone. This attitude will produce a feeling — that's aspiration. Aspiration is what we desire, and this desire will move us to the next step — action. It is our actions, what we do, that will bring forth our accomplishments, what we get.

IT IS THE APPLICATION OF WHAT YOU LEARN, THAT WILL DETERMINE WHAT YOU EARN.

There is a certain amount of truth in the expression "knowledge is power." The true power lies in the application! It is the application of what you learn that will determine what you earn. Anyone who attended the first grade knows what two plus two is. However, when asked the question in a classroom, how many will be ready to go and write the answer on the blackboard. Knowing the answer is not enough. You will have to get up and show what you know.

Neosporin is an ointment utilized to help treat minor cuts and burns. If you cut yourself or scrape your arm, simply knowing what and where the Neosporin is will not nurse the wound. The wound will not begin to heal until the Neosporin is applied. The application must take place.

We live in a society driven by information. Therefore, the amount of information one has is directly proportional to the amount of information one can apply. For example, salaries for those working in the educational system are based on how much education an individual has obtained prior to applying for the position. The theory is that the more education one has, the more value one has to the system.

> "Always do right - this will gratify some and astonish the rest."
>
> *Mark Twain*

THE SCHOOL BOARD OF BROWARD COUNTY, FLORIDA
2007-08 INSTRUCTIONAL SALARY SCHEDULE

Standard Broward County Florida School System Salaries

YEARS OF EXP	LEVEL	SALARY			
0	1	38,500	Master's Degree additional $3,650	Specialist Degree additional $6,800	Doctorate Degree additional $8,000

The above illustrates that there is a direct relationship between the application of what you learn and what you earn. It is important to understand that the more you earn the more responsibility you have, so you must be prepared. That brings us to Principle #8.

If people like you they'll listen to you, but if they trust you they'll do business with you.

Zig Ziglar

IT IS BETTER TO BE PREPARED FOR AN OPPORTUNITY AND NOT HAVE ONE, THAN TO HAVE AN OPPORTUNITY AND NOT BE PREPARED FOR ONE.

Success is all about preparation. Even when we were in school, the only way to get to the next grade was if you passed the grade you were currently in. The sixth grade is designed to prepare students for the seventh grade. Most individuals have a spare tire in the trunk just in case they get a flat tire. It is better to have a spare and not need it, than to need a spare and not have it. So it is in life.

We often ask for blessings we are really not prepared to receive, and because we are not prepared, we don't know what to do when we receive them. For example, we want a raise because we want more money. However, when we get the raise, we continue being careless and remain in financial peril because we have not taken the necessary steps to learn about money management and finance.

Most great athletes prepare for the upcoming season during the off season. They don't wait until training camp begins to start training. They begin training when everybody else is doing other things contrary to becoming great. Therefore, they come to training camp with an advantage.

During the summer months, kids are out of school and enjoying themselves. However, you have some kids who are not only enjoying summer recreational activities but are also going to activities that teach them to accomplish something as well, such as computer camp or working a summer job. It is the individuals who take time to go the extra mile who become extraordinary individuals. If it is success you desire, get prepared. It is on the way. Be patient while being persistent. Make sure you prepare for your blessing!

LEARN THE GAME OF ECONOMICS

Our society is based on economics, the selling of goods and services. There are two positions when it comes to the game of Economics: Consumers and Producers. Consumers are individuals who spend a majority of their money on goods and services. To a large degree, our society was set up to make us dependent on spending money. For example, we all need items such as toothbrushes, toothpaste, soap and deodorant. All of those items are necessary for us to live in a healthy and respectable manner, and we are forced to purchase them. Our purchases make us consumers. Everything we buy is produced by some company or individual, this makes them producers. Producers become wealthy because they provide goods or services consumers need. All of us are Consumers in some shape, form, or fashion. Even when the Producers are Consumers, they are buying some of the goods and services that they produce, so they are paying themselves. If you truly desire to become wealthy, you must produce something. It is when one produces something that society needs or wants that one creates income streams that lead to wealth. Find a way to become a Producer versus just being a Consumer.

"Would you like me to give you a formula for success? It's quite simple, really. Double your rate of failure. You are thinking of failure as the enemy of success. But it isn't at all. You can be discouraged by failure or you can learn from it, So go ahead and make mistakes. Make all you can. Because remember that's where you will find success."

Thomas J. Watson

ATTITUDE OF GREATNESS

*I*t's important to strive to be at the top of your game by developing an "I may not be great in all things, but in all things I will try to be great" type of attitude.

Regardless of your environment or situation, your attitude should always reflect striving for greatness. Your attitude has a lot to do with your altitude. A good attitude may get you in the door, but your production is going to keep you there. A positive attitude has a definite impact on your success. An Attitude of Greatness is like wearing an undershirt that has "Attitude of Greatness" written on it. No matter what garment you put over it, the Attitude of Greatness undershirt goes with you everywhere you go. If you take off the shirt you wear to work and put on the shirt that you wear to play basketball, that Attitude of Greatness undershirt is still with you. This Attitude of Greatness undershirt is to be worn everywhere you go. Nobody is great at everything they do, but that does not mean one should not strive to be great at everything one does. Having an Attitude of Greatness is one of the keys to Success.

"The best job goes to the person
who can get it done without
passing the buck or coming
back with excuses."

Napoleon Hill

STRUGGLE DOES NOT MEAN FAILURE!

onditioning was a big factor in preparation for the upcoming season for the Men's Varsity Basketball Team at Florida Memorial University. Every morning we would wake up at 5 a.m. and run two miles on the field and do aerobics with our strength coach in the gymnasium before going to class. Then, later, we had practice at 4:30 p.m. That routine was a struggle for me until I realized that the conditioning was preparation for what was to come. We were an undersized Historically Black College, but we had a lot of heart. We did not know the word quit, because quitting was not an option. If we lost, we lost. But the loss was not because of a lack of effort. It is OK to lose, if you have given it your all, because sooner or later your effort will pay off. I began to realize that the better condition I was in, the better I played. Therefore, my future was in my hands. Make sure you realize that your future is in your hands as well. Learn to appreciate the struggle! For it is the struggle that brings growth. We know that suffering produces perseverance; perseverance, character; and character, hope. Romans 5:3.

WHEN YOU GET A SHOT, TAKE IT!

*Y*ou can't succeed without first trying. You have to be willing to take the shot.

The best way to illustrate this point is by a personal example. As I mentioned earlier, I played varsity basketball at Florida Memorial University in 1991. My playing time as a freshman was limited because of the number of upperclassmen on the team. We only carried two freshmen, Reggie "Georgiaboy" Carter from Albany and me. Coach Parker named me "Moonwa," because he said I thought I was so smooth and called Georgiaboy "Franswa" because Coach Parker gave everyone a nickname.

Being a freshman was a humbling experience. We had to carry the upperclassmen's bags on road trips, when we went to the hotels we performed room service duties, and we even had to get baldheads. However, on the court, the upperclassmen knew I was someone they had to deal with. I did whatever I had to do to be a part of the team. I was not afraid of the challenges I faced on the court, because of the challenges I had already faced and overcome off the court.

Coach Parker knew I danced to a different beat, but that was OK, because he knew I could dance. I was not a great basketball player, but when I played, I played hard. Coach liked my attitude towards the game. He understood I was not going to cheat him, because I did not want to cheat myself. My game was never about Coach. It was about my teammates and me. When I cheated during practice, it did not hurt Coach Parker, it hurt my team and me. Why? Because I was not functioning at my fullest potential.

You Can't Cheat The Game Of Life.

One Saturday evening, during my sophomore year, Coach Parker looked down towards the end of the bench and yelled out, "Hardge, go and replace Cheese," a teammate from New York. As I approached Coach to enter the game, he looked me square in the eyes and said," "Now Hardge, don't you go out there and start shooting the ball as soon as you touch it. Let the game come to you." My response was, "Yes, sir," but deep inside I knew, at the first opportunity, I was going to shoot.

Brian Palmer was the starting point guard from Miami Edison High School and was bringing the ball up the court. Once he passed half court he called the play and passed me the ball at the top of the key, and everything appeared to come to me in slow motion. When I caught the ball, it seemed as if time began to slow down. I immediately caught the ball and looked towards the rim. The next instance I heard someone in the stands yell, "Shoot-It-Hardge" and I did. Swissssh!!! That was a defining moment in my life. From that point forward, at every home game, whenever I touched the ball, people in the stands would yell "Shoot-It-Hardge." Sometimes I did not want to shoot, but when I heard them yell my name, I shot the ball anyway. I was the talk of the campus, and the students started saying to me "Shoot-It-Hardge" every time they saw me. I could be on the other side of the campus and someone would yell "Shoot-It-Hardge." That made me feel good. Even when we went on road trips and played teams in other states, individuals in the stands whom I didn't even know would yell "Shoot-It-Hardge." I still wonder who told them about me.

That's how I became known as "Shoot-It-Hardge," a nickname that stuck with me throughout my college career. Even today, when I return to Florida Memorial University for homecoming, some of students and faculty see me and say, "Shoot-It-Hardge."

What this taught me is that in order for me to make the shot, I first had to take the shot. So it is with life. Often times we are in the position of pulling the trigger that may unlock the door to us living a fuller more complete life, and we don't shoot. Being one of the better players on the team had its advantages. True, I had a shooting problem, but not only did I shoot the ball at the worst moments you could possibly imagine, I also played good defense and kept a winning attitude, probably my saving grace. My senior year I had the opportunity to call the plays, and I called my play often. I still didn't hit all my shots, but I was never afraid to shoot. When you get a chance to take a shot, take it. Just make sure you can deal with the consequences of missing. Remember, the real risk in life is to take no risk at all!

"Obstacles don't have to stop you. If you run into a wall, don't turn around and give up. Figure out how to climb it, go through it, or work around it."

Michael Jordon

of hundreds of people about how they could become financially independent? I would! Envisioning myself speaking at these meetings was a constant for me. I replayed the mental picture in my mind over and over and over again, because that is what I had a desire to do. The picture was so vivid and clear that it forced its way into reality. Every individual becomes what they are due to the dominant thought that they allow to occupy their mind.

Earning is directly proportional to applying what you learn. Adopting the mindset of a multi-millionaire was easy for me because I was always smart, and I had envisioned myself having a shipload of money from an early age. I didn't want the money just to horde for myself, but to let others know that God gave all of us the ability to get wealth (Deuteronomy 8:18). Since he gave us the ability, we may as well utilize our abilities to get it, and enrich his Kingdom.

I still was teaching, it was just teaching a different subject. Instead of teaching computers and basketball, it was wealth, prosperity, and abundance via the deregulation of the telecommunications industry. Bigger than anything, I found my gift for teaching, which led me to my purpose for living. ACN did not provide the financial reward for me, but it prepared me for the financial reward. It taught me the importance of having a positive relationship with God, people, and money. I began reading books on successful people and attending wealth seminars. The topics of prosperity and wealth were common in our organizational meetings, and we shared our dreams and desires often because we believed in ourselves and each other.

In December of 1998, I was hired as a Customer Service Analyst III by Education Technology Services, (ETS) the Technology Department within Broward County Public Schools. My starting salary was $42,000 per year, and that was a $12,000 increase from my teaching salary.

I was appreciative to get the position. However, it was not until dividing $12,000 by 12 months in a year did I realize it was only an additional $1,000 a month. Big dreams and aspirations would not let me get comfortable. Thankful, but not fulfilled, appreciative, but not settling, was my motto.

Working at ETS under the direction of Kathy Collins and Dr. Jeanine Gendron was rewarding. My primary responsibility was to assist Regina Ferrazzo with the Technology Liaison Contact Program. A few years later, Regina was transferred to the Human Resource Management Systems Department, and my title became Technology Liaison Contact Coordinator.

Every professional boxer realizes that training is a significant part of being great.

We must make sure our daily activities are directly proportional to our goal. Our lives are filled with opportunities for us to live the life we dream of. However, we have to be willing to do what it takes to live it. Where are you going? Have you chosen a direction for your life? Pick a direction and take it, but don't fake it!

IT TAKES AN INVESTMENT, TO MAKE A PROFIT

The first law of thermodynamics is that you can't get something from nothing. There also seems to be a law of human nature that says the more difficult something is to obtain, the more we seem to want it. Perhaps that's why so many of us play the lottery. The odds of winning a state lottery are about 1 in 14 million. Still, we buy lotto tickets against heavy odds in an attempt to gain instant wealth. If the amount of effort devoted towards becoming wealthy is simply going to the store, choosing some numbers dreamed about the night before and purchasing a ticket against those odds, then chances are you are not going to become wealthy. If spending a dollar is the maximum amount of effort one is going to utilize to accomplish one's dreams, then you have just displayed how much your dreams are worth to you. Keeping a bird's eye view on your dreams and having a purpose for living should not be based on one dollar. Working towards dreams and defining one's life are ambitions worth more than any lottery can pay out. Our external lives are often a representation of our internal attitudes and thoughts. Whatever it is you want in life you can achieve, but you must be willing to make the investment. You must plant a seed to reap a harvest. Now that's Bible!

Always monitor what is going on inside of you because it will manifest in your life. What you did yesterday brought you to where you are today, and something was wrong with that bird. So it is with us being successful. The mere fact we are alive gives us the opportunity to accomplish whatever we are willing to pay the price to accomplish. Nothing is impossible. The word impossible means I'm Possible.

For we can do all things through Christ, who strengthens us
(Philippians 4:13)

At the beginning of 2007, the real estate market was not doing as well as we had anticipated, and I found myself back at the drawing board. From 2002 to 2007 real estate was my bridge over trouble waters. By November 2007, it seemed as if the bridge had run out and nobody had warned me. I had several pieces of property that I decided not to build on because so many homes were going into foreclosure and it was getting difficult for buyers to secure financing. Hundreds of banks went out of business, and that had a significant impact of my business. Real Estate will always be a part of my financial portfolio, but I was at a point in life where I needed some immediate changes. As things got progressively worse I began writing Prescription for Success and recording the musical aspect of the project. By the Summer of 2008 my book and the CD were ready for the world. When things get tight, we are often squeezed into positions that are meant to bring out the best in us. There is an old adage that says "When the going gets tough, the tough get going." Remember, in order to grow through life, you must change. Your Life Cycle has a stage in it called the Cocoon; this is where the metamorphosis or change takes place. Embrace this phase of life, because this is where you will get your wings to fly.

Even though I was no longer in business with Reggie and Erik Kennon, the relationship we established back then created a bond that ventures beyond business, and that bond is based on a common purpose. They are currently involved in Tahitian Noni and doing very well working with Robert Dean, Herchell Gibbs, and Barry Bird. We were in ACN together years ago, and they stayed with multi-level marketing and finally made it big.

Robert Dean is the brainchild behind TOPGUN International, an affiliate of Tahitian Noni International, and is one of the leading money earners in the company. Mr. Dean wrote a book called, *The Dean Effect* and recently created his own Success Magazine. The magazine chronicles the Success his organization is having by utilizing Tahitian Noni International as a vehicle to create healthy and wealthy lifestyles.

I AM

INFORMATION+APPLICATION=MANIFESTATION

*I*nformation is the single most important aspect of our society. Education serves to provide individuals the proper information in various subjects so they can make informed decisions. This is truly where success begins, for without the proper information you will not achieve the proper manifestation. Once you have the proper information, you need the proper application to render the proper manifestation. This principle is simple, yet profound. I am what I know and can apply. If we knew what Donald Trump and Robert Kiyosaki knew, and did what they did, we would have what they have. However, the reason we don't have what they have is that we don't do what they do, because we don't know what they know. It all begins with what one knows, Information.

It is the application of what I know that determines what I am. It is that which was planted that is creating the results. The only way to change the result is to change what was planted. Get your shovel and start digging out the roots of unproductiveness in your life and replace them with seeds of productivity (such as success books, successful role models, CDs, DVD's, etc.), seeds of positive thinking, seeds of preparation, planning and leadership. Everything we read, watch or listen to is a seed. The only difference is the type of seed being planted.

UNDERSTAND THE DIFFERENCE BETWEEN ACHIEVEMENT VS. ACTIVITY

When working toward goals, it is important not to confuse Achievement and Activity.

Achievement is defined as the end results of action steps taken in order to accomplish a goal or objective. Activity is simply non-specific action or movement. In most cases, achievement is the end result of careful planning, hard work and dedication. Activity constitutes motion that does not need a cause.

It is easy to see the differences between a bicycle and a stationary bike. One is mobile, the other is not. Both are designed for exercising if exercise is your goal. However, the moment the goal is changed from exercising to running an errand, say going to the post office, it becomes easy to see which piece of equipment is built to get you there. This example is easy to see, but can you visualize the various aspects of your life where you are generating plenty of movement, but no achievement?

Can you recognize the activities in your life that are not getting you the results you desire? It's time to get off of the stationary bike and onto the bicycle that can take you where you want to go. Otherwise, you're simply exercising and going nowhere. Plenty of people are very busy, but their busyness may not equate to productivity. You have to make disciplined, concrete decisions

Your time is the most valuable commodity you have. When you waste your time, you are wasting your life. Life is defined as the time spent during this human experience.

"People with goals succeed because they know where they're going."

Earl Nightingale

"The spirit, the will to win, and the will to excel are the things that endure. These qualities are so much more important than the events that occur."

Vince Lombardi

THE MOST IMPORTANT INVESTMENT YOU CAN MAKE IS IN YOURSELF!

uccess and education are interwoven like red and white corpuscles in blood flowing through veins to sustain life. Acquiring knowledge and the application of what one knows is the foundation of achievement. Nobody knows everything. The definition of a smart person is not someone who knows everything, but someone who knows where to find everything they need to know. Education is the cornerstone of our civilization, so you must read to succeed.

Each day is filled with situations that create idle time, such as having to wait in a grocery line or at the doctor's office. Those situations provide a perfect opportunity to take action toward achieving your goals. Take pocketsize books with you everywhere you go to turn idle time into productive time. Books aligned with your goals that provide the mental nourishment necessary to continue moving forward will turn idle time into the most productive time of your day.

A car will not operate on its own power without any gas. A body will not continue to function or even exist without steady nourishment. Likewise, dreams need to be constantly nourished in order to be transmuted into reality. Success occurs only through preparation. The two most important features involved in the growth of your success is the management of time and applying what you learn. Your time is valuable, and reading is one of the best ways to make the most of it. Just make sure what you read can assist you in accomplishing your goal.

If You Think You're Beaten

Kristone

If you think you're beaten, you are,
If you think you dare not, you don't.
If you'd like to win, but think you can't,
It's almost for sure, you won't.

If you think you're losing, you've lost.
For out in the world we find -
Success begins with a person's will,
It's all in the state of mind.

If you think you're outclassed, you are,
You've got to think high to rise.
You have to stay with it,
In order to win the prize.

Life's battles don't always go,
To the one with the better plan.
For more often than not, you will win,
If only you think you can.

My Letter For Success

The Tree of Success will bear many fruit. In all actuality, the fruit is a manifestation of the root. Therefore, one must concentrate one's efforts on that which will create what one sees. The elements, perfections and imperfections will be seen at the proper time and in the proper season. We must concentrate our efforts on the roots of our Success.

For it is the elements within the root that will manifest into the fruit.

Pay attention to your seeds!

for whatsoever a man soweth, that shall he also reap.
Passage Galatians 6:8

Let's Get It!

Sincerely,

Mr. Hardge

CIAO!

SUCCESS TEST

Here is your chance to determine how Successful you are at remembering the vital aspects of each Success Principal by answering the following questions. If you have any problems answering the questions, you can go back and review as needed.

1. According to Success Principle #1, define Integrity.

_____

2. According to Success Principle #2, fill in the blanks.
What we _____ our time to on a daily basis,
will _____ what happens tomorrow.

3. According to Success Principle #3, Matthew 7:7-8 states

_____

_____

4. According to Success Principle #4, GIGO stands for?

_____

5. According to Success Principle #5, fill in the blanks.
People don't _____ to fail, they _____ to plan.

6. According to Success Principle #6, fill in the blanks pertaining to A-Box Theory. Your Attitude, what you _____, will determine your Aspirations, which is what you _____, will determine your Actions, which is what you _____, which will determine your Accomplishments, which is what you _____.

7. According to Success Principle #7, fill in the blank.
It is the _____ of what you learn, that will determine what you _____.

8. According to Success Principle #8, complete the following statement.
It is better to be prepared for an opportunity and not have one, then

_____ .

9. According to Success Principle #9, what are the two positions in the game of economics? _____ and _____.

10 . According to Success Principle #10, fill in the blank. " I may not be Great in all things, but _____ .

11. According to Success Principle #11, Romans 5:3 states: _____
_____

12. According to Success Principle #12, my nickname in college was
_____.

13. According to Success Principle #13, complete the statement. To be extremely successful, one must be willing to do what others _____ _____ _____, in order to have what others _____ _____.

14. According to Success Principle #14, complete the following statement. You must _____ on your ideas _____, if you want them to _____ in your life _____.

15. According to Success Principle #15, define opportunities.
_____
_____

16. According to Success Principle #16, explain the difference between Activity and Achievement. _____
_____

17. According to Success Principle #17, a smart person is defined as? _____
_____

If you are pleased with your results, then you are successful. If you are not pleased with your results, take the test again until you are pleased with your results. You are the only person who can determine your Success.

For more Information, Contact

Mr. Hardge
success@mrhardge.com
Distinct Publishing
954-336-7566
www.mrhardge.com